**Schools of the Future:
Best Design Practices**

Le Penhuel & Associés architectes
Foreword Philippe Meirieu / Interviews Alice Dubet
Illustrations Quentin Vijoux

PARK BOOKS

(RE)INVENTING THE "SCHOOL AS HOUSE"
PHILIPPE MEIRIEU

Contrary to widespread belief, it was not Jules Ferry but François Guizot who laid down the organisational and operational principles of the French school system. True, in 1882 and 1883 Ferry passed the laws that anchored education to the republican project by instituting compulsory education together with free and secular public schools; but it was Guizot – a resolute opponent of the Republic and of universal suffrage – who had previously laid the foundations of the system we are heir to today. It was in the law of 1832, under the July monarchy and Guizot's Ministry of Public Instruction that we find, for the first time, the obligation for communes of more than 500 inhabitants to open a primary school – at least for boys – and the creation of a Normal School in each département to ensure uniform training for all teachers, and to establish inspection bodies responsible for checking that teachers were applying the instructions of the newly created "official bulletin".

Furthermore, it was Guizot who settled the "quarrel of models" and endowed France with a "school type" that it would inevitably export widely via its colonial conquests. What did this involve? In the early 19th century, the French school system was not really unified. While the preceptorship method was fairly widespread among the aristocracy and the upper middle classes, there were still some remnants of the medieval model for the children of the common folk: teachers, most often in old agricultural or craft premises, provided some sort of ongoing basic teaching through personal contact rather than classes as such. There were, however, a few groups essentially made up according to the "school fees" paid by the parents. This model was clearly doomed in the very short term, being both unfair and inefficient. On the other hand, two other models appeared and rapidly gained ground: the mutual and the simultaneous.

The simultaneous model is due to Jean-Baptiste de La Salle who, at the end of the 17th century, founded the Christian Brothers. Anxious to provide free education to children who could not attend the expensive Jesuit schools of the time, he recruited teachers ready to devote their lives to God by teaching poor children. With them, he opened schools obeying three fundamental principles of solidarity: instruction was no longer given in Latin but in French; lessons were no longer given individually but in front of a class; and classes were to be made up of pupils capable of receiving the same instruction simultaneously. Schools thus began to be structured into different units of children of relatively homogeneous ages and levels. Initially there were three classes, then, at the request of teachers always keen on greater uniformity, classes gradually came to coincide with the years of birth.

With the retrospective illusion that comes so readily, it might seem that this "self-evident" model was easily imposed. Such was not the case, for alongside the simultaneous version, another model had appeared: the mutual, introduced by Scotsman Andrew Bell and Englishman Joseph Lancaster towards the end of the 18th century. Bell explained that he had come up with the idea during a mission to India, while Lancaster advocated the doctrine of mutual aid promoted by the Quakers. In the mutual schools, pupils were assigned to groups sometimes exceeding a hundred and organised, for each subject (reading, writing, arithmetic, geography, etc.), into eight "rows", ranging from the most advanced pupils, whatever their age, to beginners. The teacher taught only the first row, with the first row pupils then teaching those in the second, the pupils in the second teaching those in the third, and so on. In the interests of order, all this was highly ritualised in huge, fully equipped rooms with appropriate furniture (small and large platforms, long tables of different sizes, slates, abacuses, notice boards, sophisticated signage, etc.) and circulation plans for pupils to follow.

Adapted in Switzerland by Grégoire Girard and in France by Charles Démia, the mutual model remained a minority approach, but was supported by a significant number of intellectuals – libertarians, protestants, mutualist activists – who saw it as a form of mutual aid that could contribute to the preparation of a more united society. Guizot, however, bent on making the school one of the major tools of "government of the minds", opposed it with all his might and imposed the simultaneous model, the only one capable, in his eyes, of containing the subversive impulses of the people by training little Frenchmen in the necessary obedience to "masters" of all kinds.

In this he succeeded beyond all hope, in that the simultaneous model was without doubt the most strikingly successful of educational innovations. Do we not hear it said at the beginning of each school year that the most important thing is "a teacher in front of each class"? The whole world seems to be convinced today that some all-powerful god once dictated to a school Moses the tablets of law imposing that, "from now on and for all eternity, every school shall be organised in groups of twenty to forty individuals, of the same age and supposedly of the same educational level, lined up one behind the other, doing the same thing at the same time under the authority of a teacher." As a result, our schools are not organised according to what our pupils need to learn and how they can go about learning it; instead they are forced into a kind of parallelogram and lined up in rows, in ranks, in "classes" – the word has been imported from botany and zoology. Many learning objectives have been sacrificed in this way, whether they relate to fundamental knowledge – reading, writing, counting, and also oral and physical expression, exploration and investigation, analysis and creativity – or civic skill – mutual aid, cooperation, discussion, deciding together on matters of the common good – or else, major cultural issues as discovering and appropriating the works of art thanks to which human beings have managed to find emancipation throughout their history.

Forgotten is the tradition of the journeymen of the Middle Ages, for whom manual work meant close focus, exploratory dialogue with resistant materials, and outdoing oneself in the achievement of a masterpiece. Today so many students struggle to internalise the requirements of precision, accuracy and truth. Forgotten are the virtues of mutual aid and the exchange of knowledge promoted by ,the mutual school, whereas research has demonstrated its immense cognitive and socio-affective benefits, as much – and sometimes even more – for the helper as for the helped. We have forgotten the extraordinary privilege African children enjoy in being able to talk freely with their elders under the palaver tree, this in spite of our awareness of the importance of intergenerational transmission and its calming and structuring functions. We have forgotten, too, the ritual of "knowledge theft" that the inhabitants of Nepal used to practise: placing fearsome guards around adult assemblies, supposedly to frighten the children, but in fact to trigger their curiosity about hidden knowledge. Around us now we see how overload and immediate accessibility kill the desire to learn. Gone are the open-air classrooms in Bhutan and elsewhere, where pupils themselves marked out their work space, built their desks and searched in nature for the materials they needed for their work. So many children today know nothing of the natural world and are so trapped in virtuality that they readily imagine that shouting at tomatoes makes them grow faster!

While there is no question of going back to these old models, which are linked to specific societal and cultural contexts, why ignore their lessons and remain stuck in a school type imposed at a given moment in our history and obviously largely obsolete today? Educationists have never ceased to denounce its arbitrary nature. In 1792 Johann Heinrich Pestalozzi, called upon to help the abandoned orphans of Stans, in Switzerland, gave up the idea of organising his teaching by classes. In an engraving of the time, we see him discussing an architectural illustration with three girls of different ages; at his feet a pupil teaches reading to children younger than herself and, next to her, children are reading while others are playing. There is no ranking here: "What's the point of tyrannising bodies," asks

Pestalozzi, "when, in any case, minds will wander?" It's better to allot tasks that mobilise pupils than to assign them to formal obedience.

In 1921 the Geneva-based educationalist Édouard Claparède wrote a decisive, still not fully appreciated work, L'École sur mesure ("tailor-made schooling") in the wake of the New Education movement that emerged after the slaughter of the First World War. His aim was a peaceful world through education: "When a tailor makes a garment," he wrote, "he adjusts it to the measurements of his client; if the client is fat or small, he does not force him to wear a suit that is too tight on the pretext that the width corresponds in theory to his height. The school, on the contrary, dresses, shoes and grooms all minds in the same way. It has nothing but ready-made clothes and its shelves do not contain the slightest choice. Why do we not offer the spirit the same consideration as the body, the head and the feet?" For all that, Claparède did not dream of putting each pupil in front of a machine that would offer him, throughout his studies, a strictly individualised education, perfectly adapted to his "personal profile" and guaranteeing success: he knew that school is not solely for learning but for learning together, with and from each other.

It was with this principle in mind, moreover, that Célestin and Élise Freinet set about building their school on a plot of woodland in Vence, in the South of France, in 1934. To ensure the children constant contact with nature, they built a house matching the unevenness of the ground, to the point of making the steps irregular "so that the child would climb them not mechanically, but consciously." The school has an open-air theatre, a swimming pool, a vegetable garden and an orchard, together with a solarium terrace and workrooms of different sizes and shapes – one for printing, one for modelling and another for drawing – and modular classrooms where the children could give "small lectures", watch films, carry out scientific experiments or work individually. The "round table" was a circular space for "the council", where one could only enter after having deposited one's "spear" – one's aggressiveness and violence – at the entrance, in order to calmly debate the common good. The canteen opened onto the kitchen, where the children were called on to work, just as they were involved in decorating and maintaining a school which thus became completely "their home".

Although often quoted, the Freinets were not really listened to: the school in Vence has remained, along with the schools installed by Le Corbusier on the top floor of his Cités Radieuses, happy exceptions, while the standardised "Pailleron-design schools" flourished all over France. Admittedly, the "school explosion" triggered by the demographic boom of the 1950s forced the State to build quickly and economically, doubtless leaving the architects of the time little room for manoeuvre. Fortunately this is no longer the case and even if the devolution of school buildings to local authorities has created inequalities that must absolutely be reduced, it has nevertheless allowed for the freeing up of initiative and a radical reversal of the equation. We are asking a little less of pupils and their teachers in terms of adaptation to a standardised school form, and we are trying to think a little more of the "school as house", allowing for the best possible living and learning conditions.

This book is a remarkable illustration of this welcome change of direction. It talks about differentiated spaces, workshop classrooms, open streets, free access libraries and playgrounds. Rotundas, alcoves, hamlets and forecourts make their appearance. Nooks and crannies are created. Classrooms are being expanded and corridors socialised. Spaces are decompartmentalised and continuities are created between interior and exterior. The openings are rethought so that the school is neither totally transparent nor completely closed off: rather it is both open to the world and centred on school work... The architectural proposals made here are not the whims of ingenious designers absolutely bent on leaving their mark. They are thought out, designed and implemented to promote the core project of our school: learning to think and to be part of society, acquiring knowledge and growing in humanity.

The architects voicing their ideas here know that "stones can speak" and that the structure and layout of a site largely determine what happens there. A child does not behave in the same way in his room as in a theatre, a train, a stadium, a library or a nightclub. This is why it is essential that children enter a school where they feel welcome and safe, where the walls themselves bear witness to the importance of the culture that we are trying to make them love, where the spatial arrangements embody the concern for precision demanded of them in their written work, where they can converse calmly with their peers in dedicated spaces, see what is happening in the kitchen, and go to the toilets without feeling embarrassed. It is essential that the whole school, in all its spaces and details, reflects the standards it seeks to transmit. Otherwise students will not inhabit it and will go on thinking that "real life is elsewhere."

INTRODUCTION
LE PENHUEL & ASSOCIÉS

How are we to design spaces that enable us to teach differently? How can architecture back up, and even put forward, innovative educational practices? With almost thirty years' experience of designing educational facilities ranging from crèches to high schools and everything in-between, Le Penhuel & Associés have accumulated invaluable expertise in the field. By sharing practical solutions and paying attention to clients' changing needs, we hope to be part of a profound and lasting overhaul of education in all its aspects.

Environmental and energy issues have transformed our ways of working and we are convinced that this is also an opportunity to reassess the way we design our schools: how are we to make the architectural project part of a sustainable approach and offer our children greater spatial inventiveness within the budgetary limits?

The intelligence of our profession must find expression in this chance to work thriftily. We need to become economically efficient by creating modular spaces that can be used in a variety of ways, and by rethinking our relationship with comfort, safety and, more broadly, the outside world. We firmly believe that controlled contact with the elements – light, vegetation, wind, rain, heat, cold – is crucial to pupils' development. These principles can be put into practice progressively when the client has educational ambitions, or more simply by injecting a few ad hoc improvements into a fairly standard programme. It's by moving away from standardisation that innovation becomes feasible again, so it's up to us to be a driving force, looking well beyond mere certification, for the virtuous school of the future.

Given the widespread adoption of environmental requirements by building owners, we now need to start thinking globally and collectively very early on. Building with wood, stone or earth means involving all the participants in the project from the competition stage onwards, so as to integrate the structural logic of each material. The pleasure of designing and building must also be sustainably reflected in the design of teaching spaces, to help society develop through education.

In all our projects we attach the utmost importance to the quality of natural light, the correct proportion of interior and exterior volumes, and the matter of textures and materials, the aim being to encourage users to make the most of the spaces we have designed for them.

When we come up with new practices, we have to take the time to explain them in advance, even if we ultimately don't decide how the space will be used. Ideally, right from the planning stage, consultation with future users will help identify their needs and wishes, enabling us to adjust the project so that, at handover time, the teaching team can take full ownership of the space.

As architects, it is through the quality of the spaces designed that we contribute to the evolution of teaching practices, and the (re)invention of the "school as house" in the long term.

A   AMPING UP THE CLASSROOM
P. 23

B   BROADENING THE BOOKS
P. 39

C   COMMUNICATING
P. 49

D   DECONSTRUCTING THE HALL
P. 51

E   EYES AND EARS
P. 61

F   FREE TIME
P. 63

G   GREENING
P. 65

H   **HYBRID COURTYARDS P. 67**

I   **I TO EYE P. 81**

J   **JUMP TO IT! P. 83**

K   **KNUCKLING DOWN P. 85**

L   **LISTENING AND LEARNING P. 87**

M   **MUTUALISING THE COVERED COURTYARD P. 89**

N   **NAVIGATING P. 97**

O	**OPENING UP THE CANTEEN**	**P. 99**
P	**PLAYING**	**P. 109**
Q	**QUESTIONINGS**	**P. 111**
R	**RECESSES, NICHES AND NOOKS**	**P. 113**
S	**SOCIALISING THE HALLWAYS**	**P. 115**
T	**TRYOUTS**	**P. 125**
U	**UNITY**	**P. 127**

V	**VISIBILITY FOR SPORT P.129**
W	WHERE, WHEN AND HOW? P.137
X	X-FACTORS P.139
Y	YOYOING P.141
Z	ZIGZAGING P.143

When a class is saturated, there's no other option than to put the pupils in rows. Circles and U-shapes, on the other hand, allow everyone to see each other, to form a group in which the teacher can be included.

AMPING UP THE CLASSROOM

Tremblay-en-France, school complex (2022–5)

AD
LP
AA Throughout their school career, from age 3 in nursery school to 17 in high school, children spend their days in a 60 m² classroom with twenty-five of their classmates. How can we improve their classroom experience? Within this limited space, it is often impossible to accommodate everyone's different uses and rhythms. For twenty-five pupils and a teacher 60 m² is barely more than 2 m² per person. The spatial constraints of the traditional classroom – children in rows of two opposite the blackboard – are very effective for face-to-face teaching, but these days many teachers are opting for a different approach by moving away from this confrontation between teacher and pupils. To open up the field of possibilities, we need to create subspaces in the classroom, allowing several types of use in the same day – work in small groups of five or six, for example – or letting a child who has finished an exercise leave his desk and go and read in the library, without disturbing his classmates.

In the course of the last century, the number of pupils per class here in France has gradually increased, while the actual surface area has remained unchanged. Is this still the right size? Isn't it time to challenge the sacrosanct 60 m²? This has happened in housing and other programmes, but the surface areas allotted to schools have changed little or not at all. We really need to understand what an extra 10 m² would allow. As French architects Lacaton et Vassal have done in the housing sector, we need to demonstrate that building bigger is not more expensive and that if we are to enable students to develop on a daily basis, we should limit their numbers – not forgetting the relief this would bring to overworked teachers in schools in priority education networks. Right now there are twenty-five pupils for two teachers per class, and they are being offered 80 m² classrooms in new buildings. This change has had a direct beneficial impact on the way they approach school. Adding 10 m² to all the newly-built classrooms would be a considerable step forward in teaching terms.

AD
LP
AA Is it the role of the architect to ask for more space and more teachers for schools? We need to say it loud and clear: this should be the norm. Looking after thirty children at a time is a very difficult job. The amount of time a teacher can spend directly with each child is very limited, and it's not always easy to spot when a pupil is in difficulty. With "only" twenty pupils to teach, it's possible again. When a class is saturated, there's no other option than to put the pupils in rows. Circles or

U-shapes, on the other hand, allow everyone to see each other, to form a group in which the teacher can be included. When, at the preliminary stage of an architectural competition, the client asks for 60 m² classrooms equipped with thirty individual desks, or fifteen desks for two, it quickly becomes apparent just how limited the surface area is. The furniture does not seem to match the plan, leading to an artificial reduction in the size of the tables. Depending on the number of pupils per class, there may or may not be space available. This is clearly one of the levers available to our institutions to improve the educational quality of classes.

AD
LP
AA

In the meantime, how do you propose to restore the potential of these square metres? The second lever is architectural: making the most of all the space available to offer users a variety of layouts and greater flexibility. Integrated furniture is useful for creating "nooks", while playing with the geometry of the space. If the 60 m² available is saturated because it is occupied by pupils and their desks, as well as by the need to circulate within the classroom, the layout becomes fixed and it's difficult to imagine any parallel use. In kindergarten, where teaching in small groups is the rule, different recesses can be created in the classroom, even if it means making certain areas denser. It's with the introduction of the blackboard from elementary school onwards that it becomes complicated to propose a fragmented space from the outset. Sub-spaces can be created using a variety of tricks that don't encroach on the rest of the classroom: by placing a window a little further back in its recess, and fitting it with a shelf, you can create a library corner at a lower cost and without using floor space.

    A classroom often has one long straight wall, offering the potential for comfortable seating for some additional use. Between two classrooms, you can also create a thick partition that incorporates seating and storage, while at the same time providing soundproofing. Moving away from the traditional rectangular room also reshuffles the space cards. When an area becomes a rotunda, for example, you realise that you're entering a dedicated space, and you can fit out different functions for it – workshops, games, a library, etc. Twenty years ago, at the Andrésy school for example, we proposed a small platform dedicated to the visual expression workshop area in the nursery classes. Recently, in Bondy, we adapted the concept to a patio. So there are a lot of clever things you can do in a classroom.

By opening it up to the room next door or to the corridor, there are even more ways of increasing available classroom space.

AD
LP
AA

Does the classroom's outreach extend beyond its spatial limits? When the number of pupils and the surface areas allocated to classrooms are unchanging, interesting use can be made of the corridors bordering them. The idea, of course, is not to open up the classroom onto a narrow, windowless corridor, but to widen it so as to create pockets – sub-spaces that can, thanks to a movable partition or a window, augment the limited space of the classroom. However, when making this choice, you need to be aware that using the circulation as an extension of the classroom, and therefore as a workspace, is not easy. In France, the classroom is sacred. Our children are expected to be good and to concentrate at their desks without moving or talking for long hours at a stretch. A challenge that we adults are often incapable of meeting ourselves! And the students are like a pressure cooker: as soon as they walk through the door, they explode. The corridor is almost playtime! So teachers are sometimes reluctant to open a breach.

AD
LP
AA

How can we get round this prejudice? For example, two or three classrooms can be opened onto a wide circulation area that they would have in common, rather than onto the main corridor. In the Île-de-France region, a school often has twenty classrooms – twelve elementary and eight nursery. The scale of such establishments can often weigh upon young children, but by dividing classes into clusters, we create small, much more reassuring communities, where pupils can quickly find their bearings. We did this at the Bondy school, which is due to be handed over at the end of 2023, and where we were faced with technical issues that sometimes pushed current standards to their limits, particularly in terms of fire safety. Traditionally circulation areas and classrooms must be separated by firewalls. But other systems exist, too, even if they are less widely used because they are more complex to design. At Bondy, we have chosen to work in compartments. The school is made up of several large units within which there is no need for a firewall barrier; this considerably reduces the thickness of the partitions, opening up new possibilities. Each "compartment" is spread over two levels, each measuring 300 m², making it easier for children to get to grips with the space. The result is three "hamlets" – small, medium and large sections – each with four

The idea, of course, is not to open up the classroom onto a narrow, windowless corridor, but to widen it so as to create pockets – sub-spaces that can, thanks to a movable partition or a window, augment the limited space of the classroom.

Østny, secondary school (2021–4)

classrooms, where internal circulation is quietened down. This counter-intuitive typology is not something project owners are used to, it considerably enriches the spaces offered to school users and creates new reflexes, while once again leaving the designer room to move.

AD
LP
AA

What happens inside the hamlets? The hamlets are organised around small planted patios, and we have proposed different configurations for each. In the first, the classrooms can meet in pairs, in the second they open onto the circulation area and in the third they can do both. Each room has two steps leading up to the "workshop", separated from the rest of the space by a low cabinet fitted with a washbasin. Between the workshops of adjacent classes, sliding and pivoting partitions allow teachers to combine their rooms to work together if needed. All they have to do is shift these movable panels, which can be stored in the side cupboards. These features were conceived at the competition stage, then developed during consultation with the future users, who found the project really inspiring. Bondy's education department grasped their importance and played along. This gradation of opening possibilities goes hand in hand with the choice of a highly flexible post-and-beam or post-and-slab structure. If, in five, ten or fifteen years from now, the City finds that one solution works better than the others, adaptation of the space will require simple modification of a partition. For the client and for us this is a new experience, and we can't wait to see how these spaces are appropriated by the teams over time.

AD
LP
AA

How much leeway does the architect have with regard to classroom furniture? When it comes to integrated furniture, clients are often quite receptive, as long as the budget is kept within bounds. We design a lot of the furniture for our schools, particularly storage units. We believe that a flexible space open to all possibilities should be free, and therefore tidy. This is also a way of orienting uses: here a small amphitheatre for a storytelling area, there a washbasin and a bench for experimentation, there again a bench and some shelves for a reading nook, etc.

But for the rest of the furniture – cupboards, desks, chairs – the contracting authority often has framework agreements with mass-market suppliers, with a view to reducing costs through economies of scale, and this often presents a stumbling block. Some municipalities, such as Rosny-sous-Bois, have their own workshops and therefore supply furniture. The cost is no higher, and the result is often of much higher quality. As architects, we really need to appropriate this task in its entirety. We insist every time that we should at least be involved in the selection process, but we sense resistance from the clients. Although they are primarily concerned about the cost, the furniture is often also a way for them to make the building their own by fitting it out, as they would do in their own homes. Unfortunately the future users are rarely given the option, and this can lead to some bizarre situations. Sometimes standard furniture ordered in excess take over the classroom, up to and including the glazed façades! When we've spent time designing the layout to save every useful square metre for the pupils, and the contractor has done a remarkable job during the building work, it's a blow to end up with premises that are all but unusable! The way the children and the teachers experience their classrooms throughout the year also involves a certain spatial culture; if the space is saturated, pupils' movements will be restricted, and the resultant noise will disturb their classmates. When the space is well-defined and organised, with proper circulation areas, the pupil regains his freedom of movement.

AD
LP
AA

Is this minimalist ideal feasible? Like a child's bedroom, it demands a lot of energy. All the more so because there is not always the same number of pupils in a class from one year to the next, or even from one week to the next: when a teacher is absent, for example, and his numbers have to be shared out among the other classes. The space and the furniture must be able to absorb these fluctuations without suffering too much. Integrating these contingencies from the design stage onwards also requires a "school culture". We know how to live in a home, because we all experience it on a daily basis, but the same cannot be said for the school. Do we remember what thirty pupils represent, scattered through a 60 m² room? As architects of this type of facility, it's our role to know the environment well and always be alert to feedback. You have to be ready to go out and observe, to experience the school in order to design it better. What's a day like in a 1930s Jules Ferry school, a 1970s open-air school or a new building? We have a lot to learn from our users.

As architects of this type of facility, it's our role to know the environment well and always be alert to feedback. You have to be ready to go out and observe, to experience the school in order to design it better.

AD
LP
AA

What about modular furniture? For a high school in Vincennes, east of Paris, we came up with multiple-configuration classrooms by using tables on castors, whose geometry made different combinations easy. Even drawing on the standard catalogue, you can choose furniture that will adapt to the space intelligently. On the other hand, when the slightest change requires too much energy, is too noisy or takes too much time, you're faced with obstacles to multiple use. Late in 2022 we won a competition for a kindergarten and primary school in Tremblay-en-France, where the client was in favour of innovative teaching methods. Modularity was one of the prerequisites, and designing the furniture was part of the architect's tass from the outset. The programme clearly stated that "the pupil should be put back at the centre of the school system." In this context, the classroom is no longer allocated to one teacher, or even one level; it must be ultra-flexible in order to accommodate all educational and extra-curricular activities.

AD
LP
AA

Educational and extra-curricular activities sharing the same spaces? There are two teams working together in primary schools (nursery and elementary): the teaching staff, who report to the Ministry of Education, and the local authority staff, in charge of administrative, after-school and catering services. They work together, sharing premises and responsibilities, but are not accountable to each other. When teachers are obliged by lack of space to share their classrooms with the after-school activities, conflict can result. To avoid this, the activities centre in many recent programmes is entirely separate. This involves four, five or even six rooms occupied only twenty per cent of the time: on Wednesday afternoons, Saturdays and during the school holidays.

At Tremblay, for example, it was specified from the outset that all classrooms were to be shared with the extra-curricular activities. This choice has enabled the developer to increase the surface area of the classrooms by almost 20 m² each! It's up to us to suggest approaches to this shared use. Even if, in this case, it forms part of the educational project to which the teachers have already agreed, it must not lead to a loss of bearings for the teams, or a form of spatial disengagement. If the sharing process is well organised – with built-in lockable storage units and modular furniture, for example – it can run very smoothly indeed.

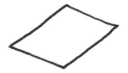

Even drawing on the standard catalogue, you can choose furniture that will adapt to the space intelligently. On the other hand, when the slightest change requires too much energy, is too noisy or takes too much time, you're faced with obstacles to multiple use.

We thought it would be more interesting to see the library as an open space extending from the hall, an extension populated by books.

BROADENING THE BOOKS

AD
LP
AA

Is the Centre for Documentation and Information (CDI) still an important aspect of school life? Indeed it is, and we systematically locate it at the heart of our projects. In the recently built secondary school in Cergy, we set the CDI on the first floor, between the covered courtyard and the triple-height hall. With its generously glazed façades and assertive centrality, it forms a volume that almost seems suspended in space. We then went on to win the competition for the Osny secondary school not far away, with a similar spatial organisation proposal. For this second project, however, we had the opportunity to meet future users through consultation workshops organised by the project owner; this had not been the case in Cergy. When it came to discussing the CDI with its young users, we realised that moving it upstairs posed certain problems. With staff numbers already reduced by the needs of break-time supervision, it is impossible to keep an eye on the whole school, especially the upper floors. Pupils can therefore no longer go to the CDI freely during break times. So, in agreement with the client, we decided to move this part of the programme to the ground floor, while maintaining the overall organisation of the plan. As a result, the offices are now on the first floor, and the CDI is at the junction of the hall, the students' foyer and the covered courtyard. We can't wait to see how users get to grips with it.

AD
LP
AA

Is it a facility that has to be locked? This change of location led us to question the library's porous nature. We thought it would be more interesting to see it as an open space extending from the hall, an extension populated by books. At the New Art Museum in New York and the Rolex Learning Center in Lausanne (SANAA, architects, 2007 and 2010), the bookshop forms a recess in the reception area. It is delimited by one or more pieces of furniture that can be closed, without reducing the available surface area. Security issues sometimes disrupt the fluidity of the space with more rigid arrangements, but this principle of decompartmentalisation is truly inspiring. Transposed to secondary schools and high schools, it encourages a view of the library as an extension of the main life space. With free access, its 200 m² enriches the daily lives of these teenagers.

    User-friendliness is another factor in ensuring sound appropriation of space. This means partial partitions to isolate certain areas, both visually and acoustically. You don't want to feel you're in the way! Although the CDI provides access to a selection of books, many students also use it primarily to work in small groups, revise or do their homework – so they need peace and quiet. We can imagine different niches, with books on one side, work areas on the other – individual workstations, communal tables – and the librarian's office nearby. The advantage here is that when the librarian is absent, his or her workstation can be closed, but the rest of the library is still accessible to the students.

There's a lot of down time in a secondary school pupil's day and at this age they don't yet have the freedom to leave the school as they please. With this open plan library, we are offering an interesting alternative to the duty room! At the international high school in Vincennes, we planned to have the CDI on the first floor above the entrance, with the books in a sort of trunk that the librarian opens and closes every day. In the programme, this was a closed room with several entrances, but the need for fluid circulation led us to open it up. As a result, the space is really occupied by students throughout the day.

AD
LP
AA

What part does the librarian play in this new spatial configuration? With the library opened up to the hall, the librarian has a very central position. No longer shut away in a silent sanctuary, most of their work takes place in the shadows and is often quite abstract for the pupils. Whence this opportunity to review their role and make them a fully-fledged pillar of the school's teaching philosophy, initiating projects that strengthen links between pupils and teachers, and providing support for pupils in difficulty. Sometimes this approach is already underway – some librarians have really made a name for themselves! – but we're convinced that architecture can help make it even better known.

It's important to point out that while almost all secondary schools and high schools have a librarian as part of their team, this is not the case for primary schools. The operation of the library and documentation centre often depends entirely on the teachers and extra-curricular teams. We became aware of this during discussions with the project management team at the Bobigny school complex. Primary school children spend most of the day in the same room, and to use the library, the whole class has to respect a time slot the teacher has booked in advance. Group inertia and organisational factors mean that this space is underused, in spite of being a significant, generally well-equipped curriculum area, because it also serves to represent the school. Wouldn't it be better, in primary schools, to dis-

Clamart, school campus / sports complex (2012–6)

tribute the extra 100 or even 150 m² in each classroom? Teachers can invite pupils of this age who have finished their exercises to sit quietly in the classroom library with a book of their choice. This encourages independence and prevents them from disturbing their classmates. Not easy adding a space like this to a 60 m² room, which is why it sometimes ends up reduced to a single shelf. With an extra 10 m² per classroom, it's possible to create a real library area, with a comfortable reading corner that can accommodate several pupils at a time. By doing this in Tremblay-en-France we gave the children immediate access to books on a daily basis, in a familiar space – a proximity to books is really beneficial to their development. Ultimately, from secondary school onwards the library as a self-contained room really comes into its own: room-swapping, timetable gaps, longer breaks and homework assignments are much more positive factors for using the library throughout the day.

AD
LP
AA

As with the playground, might we consider opening the library to the public? In the Bondy school complex the initial plan was for the library to be open to pupils and their parents at weekends and during the holidays. So we located it between the two halls and made it completely autonomous, with its own sanitary facilities and systems blocking access to the rest of the school. Finally, though, the need for a local council employee on the spot prevailed over this option for the time being. In the long term, if the project owner changes his mind, all it will take is a few events to make it a terrific facility, serving the whole neighbourhood and the local community. As with the oasis courtyards, these linking factors help to simplify the relationship between pupils and their families and school.

Primary school children spend most of the day in the same room, and to use the library, the whole class has to respect a time slot the teacher has booked in advance. Group inertia and organisational factors mean that this space is underused.

COMMUNICATING

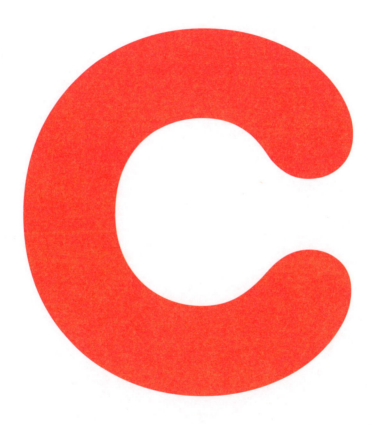

49

Traditionally the hall is a space for representing the school to the outside world. Often devoid of any built-in quality, it is from our point of view purely distributive, lost space.

DECONSTRUCTING THE HALL

Cergy, secondary school / gymnasium (2018–22)

AD
LP
AA

What's the purpose of a school hall? Traditionally the hall is a space for representing the school to the outside world. It expresses the school's status and serves as a spatial indicator for occasional visitors; it has very little to do, though, with the school's main users, in contact with it for only a few minutes a day as they enter and leave. Often devoid of any built-in quality, it is from our point of view purely distributive, lost space. Moreover, it is very poorly defined in the official building programmes, in which its surface area is given only as an indication. We plan to exploit this implicit flexibility to create more rewarding spaces, by allocating its precious square metres to other elements of the programme, more involved in the day-to-day running of the establishment.

We have implemented this approach in several of our secondary schools, notably in Cergy and Osny in the Val-d'Oise region. Both schools are organised around a large central vessel, a triple-height atrium that functions as both hall and circulation area. We reached this solution in order that the square metres gained would really benefit the life of the school. The teaching rooms are spread out on either side, as are the offices and the library. When you leave your classroom, even on the second floor, it's easy to find your way around: you can see the whole school directly from the corridor. This generous expansion gives the building unity, making the hall a meeting point and a place of assembly. And because it can be easily supervised, it gives teenagers greater autonomy. As soon as you enter the building, you are struck by the scale of this structuring space. The city is left outside. This decompartmentalisation is at the heart of our work. In our view, it considerably enriches the whole, without obtruding. In this form the boundaries of the hall are blurred, allowing it to be used throughout the day.

AD
LP
AA

What helps make the hall more than just a zone of transition? Contributing factors include its spatial, acoustic and lighting qualities, but also its layout. The Ørestad high school in Copenhagen (3XN, architects, 2007) is an impressive example, with its monumental hall that can be used by pupils in countless ways. As in Bobigny, we get a kick out of the tiered lecture theatre, with its wide range of possibilities: you can sit there to read on your own, group together in twos or threes, or use it as a gallery or meeting place. At Vincennes, we also opened up the student lobby to the hall: rather than designing a closed room, we decided to treat this as a sub-space of the central building.

D   **DECONSTRUCTING THE HALL**

As a living space entirely for the use of teenagers, it is also a means of initiating appropriation of the rest of the hall.

AD LP AA The lobby is usually at the entrance to the building. What about the interface between the street and this large vessel? In our projects, the interface takes the form of an outdoor forecourt. The entrance is in a sense externalised, extending out to form a buffer between the city and the large central atrium. Open to the sky or partially roofed in, this secure space belongs to the school, welcoming and screening all the pupils. Once through the entrance door, you're immediately caught up in the overall movement. Where the piece of land allows, direct access to the schoolyard is provided from the outside. At Cergy and Osny, the forecourts are large gardens linked to the public space. These planted areas provide a smooth transition for pupils from the hustle and bustle of the street to the interior of the school.

AD LP AA So these are also distancing devices? Yes. Vegetation, particularly in the form of planted channels, helps to distance the school from the outside world. When designing schools, the issue of security very quickly enters the equation. There have been several attacks in recent years, and the school community is worried. The hall is of special interest in this context, as it is both a point of entry and the only space where transparency is accepted by the owners. The rest of the school must not be visible from the public space, in order to protect pupils and staff.

AD LP AA If the hall is "alive", and there are uses planned for it, what about this exception in terms of safety? In schools where we've designed the hall as a large central vessel, it is always set back from the street. We feel that this configuration is essential if the hall is to be fully claimed for. In Cergy, for example, the urban master plan required the secondary school to be located on the edge of the boulevard. In consultation with the client, we decided to locate the offices and library there, to create a buffer with the rest of the programme.

In Bondy, the halls of the nursery and primary schools, with their large windows, open directly onto the street. This is also where the shared library is located. The school is on a secondary thoroughfare, and we have provided a small public square at the entrance to create a distance between the town and the building. In spite of this, we had to defend this transparency to

Tremblay-en-France, school complex (2022–5)

the representatives of the Prefecture at the safety committee meeting. Ultimately the inclusion of surveillance cameras got us a favourable decision. Hard to believe, but sometimes it's the cameras that give us a degree of spatial freedom in a system which, when it advocates total opacity, becomes almost a threat to freedom. Even the client, who supported our proposal because they wanted a "different" project from the outset, couldn't guarantee that the glazing wouldn't be covered with window sticker in the long term. These opaque plastic films are often the answer to everything, but applying them to all the ground floor glazing is not a miracle solution. In winter, they don't prevent views from outside when the inside is lit, and above all they create a shut-in feeling. It's up to us architects to be inventive and find a happy medium between a transparent school and a "blind" school, with the comfort and safety of pupils as our primary objective. An all-out focus on safety tends to make schools more inward-looking, putting parents and the general public at an even greater distance. If the school's relationship with the city is reduced to a blind interface, society as a whole becomes disengaged.

It's up to us architects to be inventive and find a happy medium between a transparent school and a "blind" school, with the comfort and safety of pupils as our primary objective.

EYES AND EARS

61

FREE TIME

63

GREENING

65

The schoolyard must be something other than a vast asphalt surface. Formerly, two or three trees were enough to embellish it: they had to be evergreen to avoid leaf collection, and without soil accessible at the foot. Today, it's almost the opposite!

HYBRID COURTYARDS

67

Chevilly-Larue, school complex (2020)

AD
LP
AA

Hasn't the playground already been reinvented? Yes, it's perhaps one of the only areas of the school that has already radically begun its transition, and has been doing so for some years now. Whatever the political persuasion of the town, there's a consensus now that the schoolyard must be something other than a vast asphalt surface. Formerly, two or three trees were enough to embellish it: they had to be evergreen to avoid leaf collection, and without soil accessible at the foot. Today, it's almost the opposite! Overall, we're still in a period of experimentation, which is exciting because it's so permissive. There have been some great successes, and some failures too. The important thing is to keep trying out new ideas before the way things are done is set in stone by restrictive regulations.

Given the age of the pupils, it's in the design of secondary school and high school courtyards that we have the greatest scope for freedom. In nursery and primary schools, it's the teachers who take it in turns to supervise playtime. The space must therefore be easy to keep under observation, whereas courtyards full of teenagers allow for nooks and crannies. It should be noted, however, that the importance of surveillance is now declining. Building owners now seem more concerned about protecting children from the outside world than protecting them from themselves. When it comes to the courtyard, they expect design proposals that are out of the ordinary, even for establishments where the programme is rather conventional.

In particular, the playground is the part of the school that has benefited most from recent attention to ecological issues. This is probably because, as an outdoor space, it can be easily transformed. From now on, the watchword is the "garden courtyard". Children, especially in an urban environment, need to be able to enjoy a quality planted area. In a school like the one in Bondy, with seventeen primary classes, you can't imagine the uproar when 500 pupils get together! The crowds are anxiety-provoking for some, and playtime becomes a dreaded moment. When the playground is made up of a single large area of tarmac, there's no escape. On the other hand, if it is divided into sub-areas, spread over several floors and planted with vegetation, it offers alternatives. Pupils then choose how they are going to socialise, whether by jumping into the deep end of a group game or sitting down with a small, quiet group. It's important for them to be able to develop outside the classroom too. Outdoor amphitheatres, previously systematically refused by building owners because they were considered dangerous, are now popular. In Bobigny, we designed a large, planted walkway where children can touch the ground, climb up and down, get together, take a tumble, etc. It's as if the threats of global warming and terrorist attacks had lessened the threat of stumbling and dirtying your hands. It's a very liberating process for children! Playtime is the freest time of their day, and it's important that they have access to a variety of spaces, so that they can develop their independence. At the same time greenery mustn't reduce play areas too much, as this would paradoxically end up working against the desired objectives. In "oasis"-type playgrounds, we need to strike the right balance between planted and open spaces.

AD
LP
AA

How did the oasis courtyard concept come about? The movement began in Paris in 2017. The capital's urban density meant that there was a real need for green spaces and, as part of a tree-planting programme – 170 000 in five years – the City council took stock of its available areas. School playgrounds were requisitioned for tailor-made redevelopment in order to "strengthen the area's capacity to meet the major climatic and social challenges of the 21st century." The City of Paris' communications drive brought the oasis courtyard national and even international visibility. Many other French municipalities, facing the same challenges, have since adopted the concept, and it wasn't long before all school design programmes were calling for their own oasis courtyard.

Oasis courtyards have a number of purposes: to provide greenery, to combat heat islands by recreating filter soil in the open air, to create play areas and quiet corners, and to offer more shade and coolness. The primary objective, of course, being the well-being of the children. Whereas the rectangular playground is very gendered – it is mainly reserved for ball games, which are often played by boys – the oasis playground is intended to be more mixed. But beyond these improvements, the scheme also involves giving the public access to these protected garden courtyards at weekends and during the school holidays. And this really makes sense! When you're a parent living in a French metropolis, where can your children play safely? Apart from a few parks, often overrun, it's hard to find play areas that are accessible to them, or where they can let off steam. In Paris, we end up in a situation where you sometimes have to wait half an hour to go for a ride on the slide. By opening up school playgrounds, especially nursery playgrounds, we

Playtime is the freest time in a child's day, and it's important that they have access to a variety of spaces, so that they can develop their independence.

are improving the quality of life of young urban children and their parents. These oasis courtyards are also new places of refuge for the elderly and the most vulnerable members of society. The recent heatwaves have shown us just how essential these cool places are in the city.

AD / LP / AA — What impact does a courtyard open to the public have on the overall design of the school? In a way we're seeing a spatial shift from the courtyard to the city. Historically the courtyard was rather protected, being surrounded by the school buildings; now it's at the interface. By designing direct access to the courtyard from the street, whether through a gate, a covered walkway or courtyard, we can hope that it will be used outside school hours. But in very dense urban areas, where the school has limited street frontage, it's not always easy to create this proximity. In any case, a local council employee must be present when the playground is open to the public, while the rest of the school does not have to be accessible. In Le Pecq, for example, we have fitted the ground floor classrooms with secure French windows and burglar-proof glazing. These devices have a certain economic impact, but nothing insurmountable. In the end, the courtyard needs to be protected during the week and open at the weekend, and it's up to the architects to seize this paradox and innovate.

In Bobigny, the school complex is located along a major avenue, in a generously treed area. The lengthy geometry of the plot led us to place the nursery school playground directly on the street. Now, even if it has to be open to the public, it is above all necessary to guarantee the privacy of the youngest children. We therefore planned to surround the school with two densely planted ditches, separated by a fence. Surprisingly, despite the non-permanent nature of the vegetation, the client accepted this proposal. The advantage of this type of arrangement is that it helps facilitate the children's relationship with the school and, more broadly, that of the residents with their neighbourhood. This acceptance is a really positive sign: everyone involved in the project clearly understands the extent to which the introduction of vegetation enhances the experience of the school and the town.

AD / LP / AA — Is the oasis courtyard only relevant in dense urban environments? No. Even in towns with a high proportion of green spaces, or in more rural areas, the oasis courtyard has many

Vincennes, international high school (2021)

advantages. Some parents feel more secure about letting their children play, and it helps to empower them. Like a park or a square, when the space is delimited, children can move around more freely. Opening the school gates outside school time is also an opportunity for pupils to show their parents where they are going, and this encourages dialogue. The school playground becomes a social space where different generations can meet and exchange ideas. In the long term, this scheme will make all citizens more aware of the importance of school.

AD
LP
AA

Can the oasis courtyard be used for other purposes? Yes. The purely recreational dimension of courtyards needs to be reconsidered. In particular, they can become perfect places for learning about biodiversity: discovering plant species, insect hotels, vegetable gardens, etc. These new uses are already appearing in the oasis courtyard but, following the example of practices observed in northern countries, we think it would be interesting to be able to leave the closed space of the classroom and teach in the open air. There are various ways of doing this, including amphitheatres, shaded clearings and pergolas.

AD
LP
AA

We're seeing more and more projects incorporating rooftop playgrounds. Do they meet a particular need? Ten or fifteen years ago, the idea of green roofs, or even living on a roof, was unthinkable. Since then we've been looking for ways to optimise the use of land and now, in almost half of our school projects, the playground is on the roof. The surface area of the playground must represent the equivalent of at least 3 m^2 per pupil, and the land allocated to schools, particularly in the Paris region, is increasingly cramped. When you add up the surface area of the building and the outdoor space, there's often a shortfall. Of course, rooftop classes of the same quality as those on the ground require more technological input, but certain situations justify it. Between the above-ground vegetation, its watering and the structure that supports the whole, they undoubtedly weigh heavily in the overall economics of the project. In Clichy-la-Garenne, the school was to be entirely of wood, but it didn't make sense to design the garden courtyard on the roof if we followed this principle: it would have created problems of water infiltration and impact noise in the premises below, not to mention the weight of the whole structure, and all at a much higher cost. And so for this area specifically, we opted for a fully optimised concrete slab-and-column structure.

Rooftop courtyards are becoming increasingly common throughout the country. Soon, as part of the ZAN (zero net artificial development) initiative, all projects, whether in urban or rural areas, will be compact and designed to save space and surface area.

A raised courtyard also poses issues of visibility. While some building configurations allow privacy to be preserved, in Clichy-la-Garenne the ground floor courtyard is within sight of the residents of the surrounding buildings, albeit from a distance. But what could be better than a playground to liven up the heart of a neighbourhood? The client, who wanted a very open school, agreed to this principle. Seeing and hearing the children in their daily activities helps to raise the profile of the school and its stakeholders.

AD
LP
AA

The playground is also where the toilets are located. Are they necessarily hidden from view? It's important to mention them here because this is often a sensitive subject in the life of a school. Although some toilets are located on different floors for use during and between lessons, they are used most frequently during breaks and lunchtimes. So 80% of them are in the playground, or connected to it. Unfortunately, as Maurice Mazalto points out in his book *Concevoir des espaces scolaires pour le bien-être et la réussite* (L'Harmattan, 2017), almost a third of pupils sometimes hold back all day to avoid having to use the school facilities. Reasons for this include insufficient numbers of toilets, which in addition are dirty, uncomfortable and offer little privacy. However, holding back can have harmful health consequences, and our children need to be able to learn cleanliness and hygiene under the right conditions. From secondary school onwards, toilets become social spaces in their own right, where they can meet up and chat away from the crowds when the playground doesn't allow it.

For safety reasons, toilets today are often built on the American model, with thin partitions open at the top and bottom. It's hard to get any privacy in there, because there's no soundproofing. In kindergarten, the partitions only reach half way up: the children can't see each other, but the adults accompanying them keep an eye on them. It's a real challenge to design spaces that respect their modesty while being safe and pleasant.

Moreover, hand-washing has been a vital part of the teaching of the very young for many years, and the Covid-19 pandemic has helped to make it an even more integral part of our daily routine. These areas are often considered to be of secondary importance, yet they are used very regularly throughout the day, and must therefore have real qualities: natural light, acoustic comfort and sound ergonomics.

The school playground becomes a social space where different generations can meet and exchange ideas. In the long term, this scheme will make all citizens more aware of the importance of school.

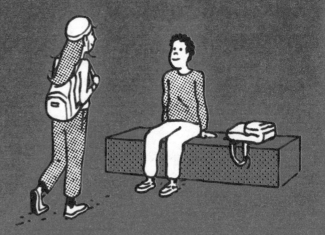

I TO EYE

81

JUMP TO IT!

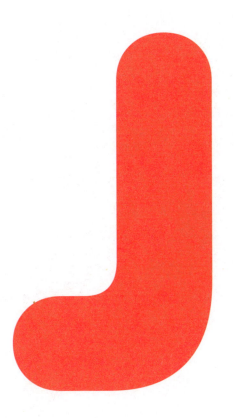

83

KNUCKLING DOWN

85

LISTENING AND LEARNING

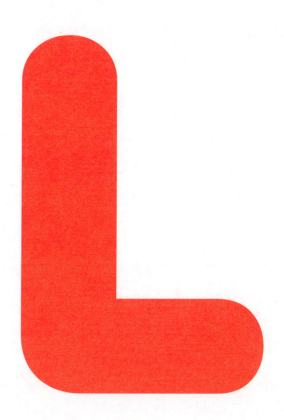

87

In most competitions, we receive programmes to be implemented on increasingly small plots of land, especially in the Paris region. Even so, we try to offer the most generous areas possible, particularly when it comes to outdoor spaces. In this complex process, it can be tempting to relegate the covered courtyard to the sidelines.

MUTUALISING THE COVERED COURTYARD

89

Osny, secondary school (2021–4)

AD
LP
AA

What exactly is a covered courtyard? It's a sheltered outdoor space, often located at the interface between the playground and the school building, which provides shelter for pupils during break time in wet weather. In summer, it also provides protection from the sun. Today, it is considered a sub-space of the playground. In fact, it is presented as such in the programmes – "courtyard: 3 000 m² including a 300 m² covered courtyard". In most competitions, we receive programmes to be implemented on increasingly small plots of land, especially in the Paris region. Even so, we try to offer the most generous areas possible, particularly when it comes to outdoor spaces. In this complex process, it can be tempting to relegate the covered courtyard to the sidelines. However, there are many ways of designing it as a multi-purpose space that can be used by everyone.

In all our projects, the covered courtyard is more than just a shelter. It is the transitional space that provides the necessary continuity between indoors and outdoors. In *collèges* and *lycées* (secondary schools and high schools), for example, we ensure that it is a direct extension of the main distributive hall, at the interface between the building and the playground. From the entrance onwards, this large panoramic volume, recessed into the building, frames the landscape and the playground. At Bondy primary school the covered courtyard is the main passageway for pupils on their way to the playground. It is positioned between the recreational elements of the programme: multi-purpose hall, city-stadium, art workshops and playground. Placing it at the junction of these structuring areas is often the most effective option for guaranteeing its daily use.

On the other hand, when the classrooms on the ground floor open directly onto the playground – like in the Bobigny and Tremblay-en-France schools – a canopy extending from the main covered courtyard provides an additional outdoor learning space. Protecting pupils from sun and rain, this extension also acts as a transition between the playground and the classrooms. Easily supervised and equipped with tables and benches, it allows children freedom of movement in the open air during lessons. Teachers can use it for messy activities, or divide their pupils into two groups – inside/outside – while keeping them within their field of vision thanks to the large windows.

AD
LP
AA

Can it expand even further? In the days of Jules Ferry-type schools, the covered courtyard was more of an indoor space with large doors opening onto the playground. It was devoted to sports and various gatherings, and had many different uses. From a thermal point of view, these schools were like open doors, and the covered courtyard was often heated despite its close relationship with the outside. The school of the future could adapt these spaces in an unheated version, still close to the courtyard but better integrated into the circulation. The covered courtyard would be an additional space, without being a room like any other. It could also be designed as a winter garden, a volume located at the inside/outside interface but protected from the wind and rain. Ultimately the idea here is to apply the housing-derived extra room principle to the school, as Lacaton et Vassal have already done at the Nantes School of Architecture (2009): a cold wall always costs less than an insulated envelope.

Completely open in summer, more closed in winter but translucent to take advantage of the sun's rays, this covered courtyard could accommodate many additional activities. Fitted with a simple thermal barrier and a removable windbreak, it can be used in all weather conditions. Be careful, however, not to end up doing away with the open covered courtyard in favour of a space that's too indoors. Our children increasingly live in highly controlled environments, and it's a good idea to maintain areas of contact with the wind, the rain and nature. After all, pupils are not going to melt! As long as they're well covered up, there's no reason why they shouldn't get some fresh air at break time, especially as our temperatures in France are mild enough for us to enjoy the outdoors without any problems for most of the year. It's simply a question of finding the right balance so that the covered courtyard retains its traditional functions, while allowing new uses to take shape.

Bobigny, school complex (2022–5)

NAVIGATING

97

By offering a choice, we're moving away from the noisy, impersonal and overcrowded canteen, and ultimately rediscovering the pleasure of eating.

OPENING UP THE CANTEEN

AD
LP
AA

What part does space play in making lunch a learning experience? The school canteen is a vital educational setting, as it alerts children to matters of taste, the importance of a varied and balanced diet, and the need for quality produce. Whatever the type of school, today's project owners are well aware of these fundamental issues and their role in forming responsible citizens. Learning how to sort waste, for example, is an integral part of the curriculum: when it's time to clear away the rubbish, the pupils become active participants, learning about the whole cycle of materials, from the vegetable garden to the kitchen and all the way to the compost heap. With these ground rules learnt from an early age, you often find children insisting that their parents apply them at home!

AD
LP
AA

What are the requirements for a school canteen? It has to be located on the ground floor with direct access to the street, to facilitate deliveries and staff access. Inside the school, the ideal situation is for pupils of all ages to enjoy access to the canteen under cover, sheltered from the rain. At kindergarten level, access should even be from the inside: it's a real hassle to get one or two hundred children aged between 3 and 6 dressed for lunch. In the canteen the youngest children are served at tables, while from primary school onwards the canteen can function on a self-service basis. At secondary school and high school level, teenagers are free to come and go as they please throughout the service, and this increases the possible spatial configurations. There are several types of canteen. In today's schools they're better described as reheating rooms, with meals being distributed daily from a central kitchen. Fortunately there are still schools that operate a real kitchen, operating with basic ingredients. This is the case in the Épinay-sur-Seine project, and the City is very proud of it. From a human point of view, and in terms of catering staff involvement, this is a real plus. Traditional cuisine means that establishments can once again take real responsibility for choosing their menus and their suppliers.

AD
LP
AA

How do you go about providing spatial qualities in the canteen? Inside the canteen, layout and furnishings create different atmospheres. This is often the largest room in the school, and we think it's important that it stays that way. Its generous size is also ideal for accommodating the school fête or other large gatherings. To make this work, all the facilities for eating in small groups need to be movable. Depending on the type of school, pupils have different degrees of autonomy. At secondary school and high school level, there is no notion of supervision at canteen time, so it is possible to provide recesses out of sight. In nursery and primary schools, we tend to create small rooms within the large one. Whatever the case, the aim is real partitions, with excellent acoustic qualities, so that people can eat in peace. In addition, in the secondary schools and high schools we have built, we offer several ways to sit down for lunch. Those who wish can eat at high tables with stools, or even around a low table. By offering a choice, we're moving away from the noisy, impersonal and overcrowded canteen, and ultimately rediscovering the pleasure of eating.

It is important for children to be able to eat in peace and in natural light, with views over the landscaped exterior. Lunchtime should be a real pause, allowing them to get free of the school environment and break up their very long school day. Of all the school areas, the restaurant is the one that opens up most easily to the city. More and more schools are offering outdoor areas equipped with a few tables, giving children the chance to have lunch outdoors. Ideally, when the plot of land is large enough, a small courtyard planted with trees should be set aside for this purpose. If there's no other option, this terrace can also be placed in the playground. At Osny secondary school, the restaurant opens onto a beautiful terrace overlooking the playground through a filter of vegetation. In our latitudes, an outdoor space can be used for a large part of the year, provided it is well oriented and protected from the wind. And what could be more pleasant than eating outdoors when the weather is fine?

AD
LP
AA

What about catering staff? We are very careful to show their work. Their hours are awkward, from six in the morning until mid-afternoon. As with the cleaning staff, their jobs are not highly regarded, even though they are responsible for the noble task of preparing our children's meals! We think it's important to foreground the work areas of the people who cook, clean and tidy up, in order to make pupils aware of their contribution. While this transparency is necessary between the kitchen and the canteen, we are also campaigning for kitchens to be lit with natural light. This may seem obvious, but at present the official programmes do not require it.

Looking beyond the lunch break, we would like the canteen staff to be more integrated into the teaching team. Our

O   **OPENING UP THE CANTEEN**

role is to encourage these exchanges spatially: in Bondy, for example, we have proposed an educational interface between the canteen and the school, in the form of a culinary workshop. This is a room that can be used by teachers or extra-curricular activity leaders, and where kitchen staff and children can meet. This gives them a better understanding of the processes involved in preparing their meals.

AD
LP
AA

Within the school itself, is it possible to diversify the uses of the catering area? At the high school in Vincennes we proposed dividing the canteen into two sections by means of a glass partition. There is now a self-service area, open only at mealtimes, where services are quickly brought together, and a "cafeteria", with free access and longer opening hours. This new configuration also means that pupils can bring their own meals. Thanks to this dual spatial arrangement, all pupils can enjoy the canteen at different times of the day, while still complying with hygiene requirements. In the long term for secondary schools, we think it would even be appropriate to draw inspiration from the lounge areas in everyday company offices. At the junction between the cafeteria and the hall, comfortable armchairs are arranged lounge-style around low tables, sometimes with the addition of glassed-in areas for group meetings. Depending on the time of day, teenagers can choose which space they feel most comfortable in, for having lunch, doing their homework as a group, or both.

Catering jobs are not highly regarded. We think it's important to foreground the work areas of the people who cook, clean and tidy up, in order to make pupils aware of their contribution.

PLAYING

109

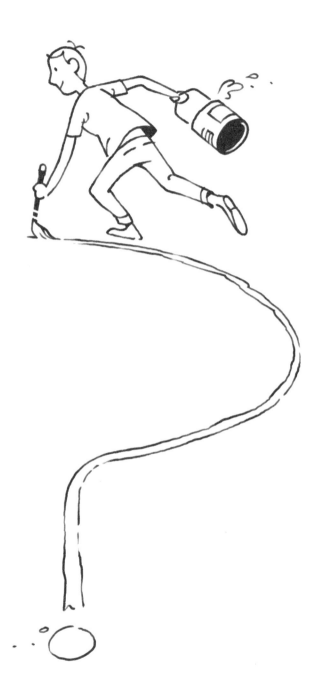

QUESTIONINGS

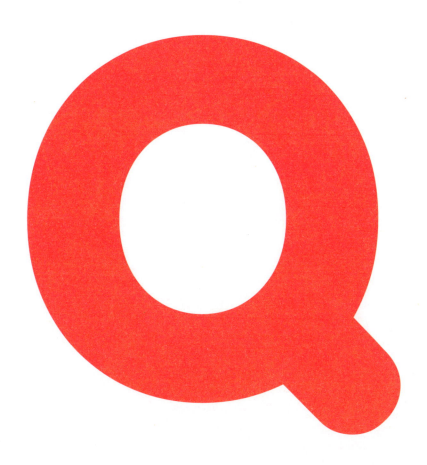

111

RECESSES, NICHES AND NOOKS

113

In a narrow corridor there's barely room to move around, and no opportunity to get together for a chat between lessons.

SOCIALISING THE HALLWAYS

115

Vincennes, international high school (2021)

AD
LP
AA

Pupils spend a lot of time in the corridors. What role do these spaces play in their learning? As well as their primary function of connecting people, corridors are meeting places. From secondary high school onwards, pupils start to move from one room to another between lessons; they become more independent, and it's in the circulation spaces that social links are forged. The architecture of these areas plays a major role in helping them learn to live together. A standard corridor is about 2 metres wide. If it is not naturally lit, or if it is squeezed between two classes, it can become a real source of friction. The corridors channel large flows of pupils over very short periods of time. Imagine thirty secondary school teenagers pouring out of a two-hour lesson during which they have been unable to move about or chat, with a very strict teacher; late for their next lesson, they're passing thirty other pupils in the same state in a narrow corridor. It only takes one of them to stop or slow down to create a traffic jam, and possibly the start of a conflict. In this limited space there's barely room to move around, and no opportunity to get together for a chat between lessons.

AD
LP
AA

How can this be avoided? Simply by widening these circulation spaces. This reduces pressure, noise levels and the explosiveness of the interclass periods. Widening the corridors reduces the risk of conflictual encounters and makes movement more fluid. To avoid building too many extra square metres, corridors can be widened at specific points, so as to create "spatial valves" or "pockets" – another opportunity to bring natural light into the heart of the school through patios or connections to the outside.

In nursery school, children are just beginning to open up to others, whereas in high school they are becoming adults. To better assist their development, we need to enhance and vary the layout according to their age, from the introverted, reassuring spaces of the early years to the generous dimensions that encourage group growth. In secondary schools and high schools we are working on the "open street" principle: the school is organised around a large double- or triple-height interior space that serves all the classrooms. The corridors merge with the hall to form a real social space, where everyone can meet and get their bearings. This is the school lobby.

AD
LP
AA

What's the point of combining the corridors with this central nave? It's a way of allotting uses to our corridors and justifying their size. Parents can have an impromptu meeting with a teacher on a sofa; a nook equipped with high tables offers an opportunity to work between two lessons; a locker area with footstools becomes a place for pupils to make themselves at home. The overall aim is to provide multi-use spaces within the corridors themselves. By sharing corridors and halls, these two structural elements of the school are given a generous amount of space. At the nursery and primary schools in Tremblay-en-France, whose ambitions in terms of educational innovation are very high, the programme specified from the outset that the corridors could have additional functions – it's up to us to imagine them!

At the Camille-Sée secondary school and high school in Paris (François Le Cœur, architect, 1930), the corridors are so vast that on each floor they cover more floor space than the classrooms! Economic and ecological reasons make such a project unthinkable today, but the uses to which corridors can be put are truly inspiring. Transposing to 2030 and retaining those generous dimensions, we learn that the "pockets" will no longer be heated spaces, but will benefit from good solar exposure and natural ventilation systems, and the classroom partitions will be thicker, to increase the inertia of the heated interiors. If you have a good thermal design office working with you, there's plenty to work with!

AD
LP
AA

Is heating an important issue? Yes. Often, when a project claims to be "different", it's because it's fundamentally questioning its circulation. The logic behind any school complex stems from a standard of comfort: you have to be able to move around the whole building in heated areas. Combined with the need for compactness and spatial efficiency, this standard leads to a certain geometry that leaves you room for social interaction. In some schools, particularly those of the Jules Ferry type, corridors take the form of open passageways. The pupils move from one room to another through unheated areas, and they're fine with that. On the other hand, this type of circulation is not suitable for a nursery school, where the children are not yet independent when it comes to putting on their coats: it's impossible for the team to dress them all and then undress them one by one to take them to the canteen, for example!

When we began to envisage all the rooms in the school linked by unheated spaces, we imagined classrooms with non-standard shapes, grouped in twos or threes. We freed ourselves from the straight line, following the example of open-air

Bondy, school complex (2019–23)

school experiments in the 1950s, or proliferating schools like Les Plants in Cergy-Pontoise (Jean Renaudie, architect) in the 1970s, and we enlarged the possibilities. The hygienic architecture of the open-air school in Suresnes (Eugène Beaudouin and Marcel Lods, architects, 1935), whose classrooms open onto the park through large accordion-shaped partitions, also remains a key reference. This direct relationship with the outdoors – with light and nature – is the ideal we want to achieve for our children today, with the added bonus of compactness.

AD **LP** **AA** How do you get users and developers to accept open corridors? Isn't that too difficult a concession? Being unheated doesn't mean being out in the open, in the rain! You have to find the right balance between cosiness and discomfort. In a way, it's a question of combining energy sobriety and spatial generosity. Not all building owners in France are ready to fully embrace this solution, but it is gaining ground. For example, much has recently been said about a school in the 12th arrondissement of Paris (Atelier Serge Joly, architects, 2024), where the client's very strict requirements in terms of reducing energy consumption were largely met thanks to the choice of outdoor passageways. Well integrated and protected, these become an additional space dedicated to teaching for part of the year. They also entail constraints, which need to be anticipated, so that users do not feel they are under pressure from the architecture of the premises. In some classrooms, for example, there might be a changing area at the entrance where you can take off your shoes and coat in the warmth. Whatever happens, these design choices must always be substantiated and explained if they are to be accepted and used to their full potential.

Following the example of open-air school experiments in the 1950s, direct relationship with the outdoors – with light and nature – is the ideal we want to achieve for our children today, with the added bonus of compactness.

TRYOUTS

125

UNITY

127

In France, whatever the age of the pupils, they spend most of their schooling sitting in class, even though we all know the benefits of physical activity for overall development!

VISIBILITY FOR SPORT

129

AD
LP
AA

Where does sport fit in at school? In France, its place is clearly too secondary. Whatever the age of the pupils, sport only takes up a few hours of their timetable each week. So they spend most of their schooling sitting in class, even though we all know the benefits of physical activity for overall development! We should be moving towards an Anglo-Saxon style of teaching – with lessons in the morning and afternoons devoted entirely to physical education – but we're still a long way from that. With a view to increasing the proportion of sport in schools, we want to integrate related facilities into architecture as far as possible.

In densely populated urban areas, sport can take place in the schoolyard, in the sheltered area, or even in the multi-purpose hall. In nursery schools, physical activity often takes place in the motor activities room, which is larger than a traditional classroom. From primary school onwards, pupils sometimes have to use a municipal gymnasium, but more and more often in new secondary school and high school building programmes these facilities are really in demand.

Given this situation, and while we wait for a real reappraisal of the place of sport in educational programmes, we need to take advantage of every possible opportunity to integrate sports and leisure activities into as many areas of school life as possible. For example, a double-height hall can be fitted with a mini-climbing wall in addition to the staircase; corridors can be fitted with running lanes; and the playground can incorporate body-building and training modules, as in the project at the high school in Vincennes.

In Clamart, we designed a major sports complex and a school campus combining two nursery schools and two elementary schools in a single project. These two programmes face each other on either side of a pedestrian walkway linking the neighbouring 1960s housing estate to a suburban neighbourhood. The client wanted a simple playground for the local children, but we used the issue of sport in the city to enrich the project. As well as a dojo, a large gymnasium and a tennis court with controlled access, the facility also features an open-air city-stadium. Directly accessible from the street, it forms a link between the sports complex and the school campus, and is a clear invitation to movement for the pupils of the latter. It's a bonus that we're convinced will act as a catalyst for the whole neighbourhood.

AD
LP
AA

Is the city-stadium really a school facility? Yes. Ideally, as we did in Bondy, it should be located at the interface between the town and the playground. This new positioning solves several problems. When the school is open, the city-stadium is closed to the public and pupils can play in the playground or on the sports field. When the school playground is no more than a simple asphalt rectangle, occupied almost exclusively by boys' ball games, some pupils will inevitably be reduced to mere peripheral observers; on the other hand, by outsourcing the sports field, the schoolyard becomes truly mixed. Excitable, retiring, sociable or timid pupils – everyone now has a choice of where they feel most comfortable spending their break. Outside school hours, the city-stadium is available to local residents, without access to the playground. This creates different degrees of openness between the school and the town – a positive context for optimising and multiplying uses.

WHERE, WHEN AND HOW?

137

X-FACTORS

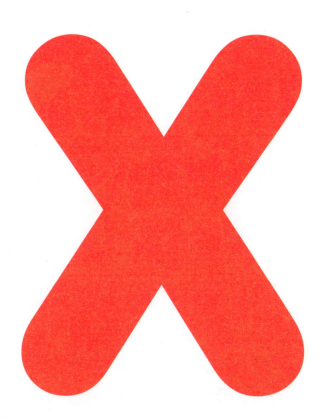

139

YOYOING

141

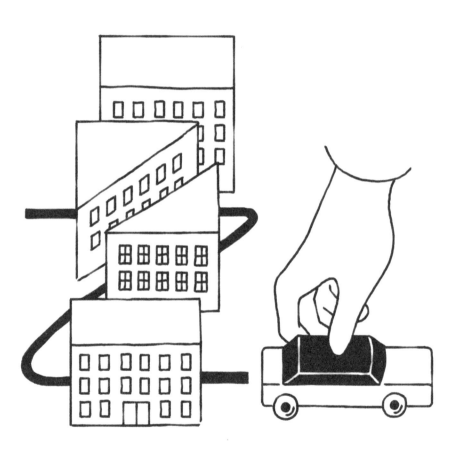

ZIGZAGING

143

P. 24
Tremblay-en-France,
school complex (2022–5)

P. 30
Osny, secondary school
(2021–4)

P. 40
Créteil, secondary school
(2005–8)

P. 44
Clamart, school campus /
sports complex (2012–6)

P. 52
Cergy, secondary school /
gymnasium (2018–22)

P. 56
Tremblay-en-France,
school complex (2022–5)

P. 68
Chevilly-Larue,
school complex (2020)

P. 74
Vincennes,
international high school (2021)

P. 90
Osny, secondary school
(2021–4)

P. 94
Bobigny, school complex
(2022–5)

P. 100
Bondy, school complex
(2019–23)

P. 104
Longjumeau, high school
(2014–20)

P. 116
Vincennes,
international high school (2021)

P. 120
Bondy, school complex
(2019–23)

P. 130
Colombes, secondary
school (2008–12)

P. 134
Clamart, school campus /
sports complex (2012–6)

Le Penhuel & Associés

For almost thirty years Le Penhuel & Associés have been practising architecture in a multidisciplinary, experimental vein. With a staff of around twenty, the practice is particularly keen on hybrid projects combining housing, public facilities, activities, shops and offices to create a generous, shared and inclusive city.

Its projects include lots O1-O3 of the Clichy-Batignolles development zone in the 17th arrondissement of Paris. It is participating in the development of the Athletes' Village in Saint-Denis and in L'Île-Saint-Denis (lots A2 and PB7) and is in charge of renovating and extending the former Renault garages on rue Amelot in the 11th arrondissement of Paris, as part of the "Réinventer Paris 2" project.

Le Penhuel & Associés are constantly challenging the evolution of the teaching facilities they have been working on for many years. This experience has brought with it real expertise in design, from crèches to nursery, elementary, secondary and high schools.

Le Penhuel & Associés feel it's now time to share its experience and convictions with as many people as possible. Aimed not only at users young and old, but also at building owners and designers, this hybrid book addresses contemporary educational spaces in order to better imagine the architecture of tomorrow's schools.

Philippe Meirieu

Researcher and education activist Philippe Meirieu has worked as a primary, secondary and vocational high school teacher and university lecturer. Initially focused on learning methods and ethics in education, he has also studied the history of educational doctrines and their impact on organised education.

He has held a number of positions in the French education system – director of the National Institute for Pedagogical Research and the Lyon Academy Teacher Training Institute – as well as in the political arena: Vice-president of the Rhône-Alpes Region with responsibility for Lifelong Education.

He is currently President of the grassroots education and training movement CEMEA. His many books – most recently *Qui veut encore des professeurs? (Who Still Wants Teachers?* [Seuil, 2023]) – have been translated into several languages.

Quentin Vijoux

This Amsterdam-based French illustrator is a graduate of the Duperré and Estienne art schools in Paris. Quentin Vijoux has worked for over ten years for various communication agencies, cultural institutions and the international press. He has published a number of books for young people and is also involved in video game projects.

Alice Dubet

An architect by training, Alice Dubet graduated from the École Nationale Supérieure d'Architecture Paris-Malaquais in 2013. She has worked as a journalist for various magazines (*AMC, Le Moniteur, L'Architecture d'aujourd'hui*), and has collaborated as author and editorial coordinator on a number of specialist books.

Acknowledgements

We would especially like to thank Building Paris, Quentin Vijoux and Alice Dubet, with whom we really enjoyed working on this project; Philippe Meirieu for his valuable time and insight; Gianluca and Gianmarco Gamberini of L'Artiere for their advice and attention to print quality; Sophie Lepolard, teacher, for her experience and commitment; the entire team at Le Penhuel & Associés for their ongoing dedication to the design and construction quality of our educational facilities; and in particular associate architects Alexandra Faucheux, Corina Laza, Warren Lepolard, João Saleiro, Pierre Soumagnac and Bruno Vaas.

We would also like to thank all the project owners with whom we have had the pleasure of working in a constant search for the best interests of users: in particular the municipalities of Bondy, Bobigny, Clamart, Clichy-la-Garenne, Pierrefitte and Tremblay-en-France; the *départements* of Hauts-de-Seine, Morbihan, Val-de-Marne and Val-d'Oise; and the Île-de-France Region. Nor should we forget all the teachers and teaching teams who work so hard every day to help our children achieve their full potential.

Credits

Editorial conception
Gaëtan le Penhuel,
Warren Lepolard,
Alice Dubet,
Camille Prandi,
Building Paris

**Art direction
and graphic design**
Building Paris
(Benoît Santiard,
Guillaume Grall,
Loïc Altaber)

Proofreading
Raphaëlle Roux

Typefaces
Karl (Source Type,
Laurenz Brunner, 2022)
Times Ten (Linotype,
Stanley Morison, 1931)

Paper
Munken Print White 90g

Pantones
Violet 525 + Rose 177

Printing
Labanti e Nanni,
Bologna, Italy

© 2024 Le Penhuel
& Associés architectes
and Park Books AG, Zurich

© for the texts:
the authors
© for the illustrations:
Quentin Vijoux

Park Books
Niederdorfstrasse 54
8001 Zurich, Switzerland
www.park-books.com

Park Books is being
supported by the Federal
Office of Culture
with a general subsidy
for the years 2021–24.

All rights reserved;
no part of this publication
may be reproduced,
stored in a retrieval
system or transmitted in
any form or by any means,
electronic, mechanical,
photocopying, recording,
or otherwise, without
the prior written consent
of the publisher.
ISBN 978-3-03860-347-4
French edition:
ISBN 978-3-03860-348-1